BOLLINGEN SERIES LXX

THE KARIYE DJAMI

VOLUME 3 *of the publication*

of an archaeological project of

THE BYZANTINE INSTITUTE, INC.

PAUL A. UNDERWOOD

THE
KARIYE DJAMI

Volume 3 Plates 335–553
The Frescoes

BOLLINGEN SERIES LXX / PANTHEON BOOKS

THIS IS THE THIRD VOLUME OF A PUBLICATION
CONSTITUTING THE SEVENTIETH WORK IN BOLLINGEN SERIES
PUBLISHED BY BOLLINGEN FOUNDATION

Library of Congress Catalogue Card No. 65–10404

Manufactured in the United States of America
DESIGNED BY ANDOR BRAUN

Contents

List of Plates

Numbers in brackets are the numbers applied by the author to the fresco subjects in the parecclesion. They correspond to the numbers appearing in red on the plans and sections and cited in brackets in the text and on the plates. The representations in the pastophoria and the sepulchral monuments are listed only by plate numbers. Asterisks before plate numbers indicate plates printed in color.

THE PARECCLESION

THE PASTOPHORIA AND PASSAGEWAYS

THE SEPULCHRAL MONUMENTS

THE KARIYE DJAMI

PLATES

The Frescoes

THE

PARECCLESION

The parecclesion. Looking east from the outer narthex

The parecclesion. Looking east

336

The parecclesion. Looking west

The parecclesion. View of the vaults, looking east

338

The parecclesion. View of the vaults, looking west

Vaults of the bema
In conch: [201]. In soffit of arch: *left*, [202]; *right*, [203]; *center*, [242].
On apse wall: *left to right*, [243] - [248]
[201] - [203], [242] - [248]

The Anastasis

[201]

The Anastasis. Detail

[201]

Ḣ ANÁTACIC

IC̅ XC̅

The Anastasis. Detail

[201]

The Anastasis. Detail: bust of Christ

The Anastasis. Detail: head of Christ

[201]

The Anastasis. Detail: Adam

[201]

The Anastasis. Detail: Eve

[201]

The Anastasis. Detail: head of Adam

[201]

The Anastasis. Detail: head of Eve

[201]

The Anastasis. Detail: hands of Christ and Adam

[201]

The Anastasis. Detail: hands of Christ and Eve

[201]

The Anastasis. Detail: the righteous at the left

[201]

The Anastasis. Detail: John the Baptist

[201]

The Anastasis. Detail: busts of the kings

[201]

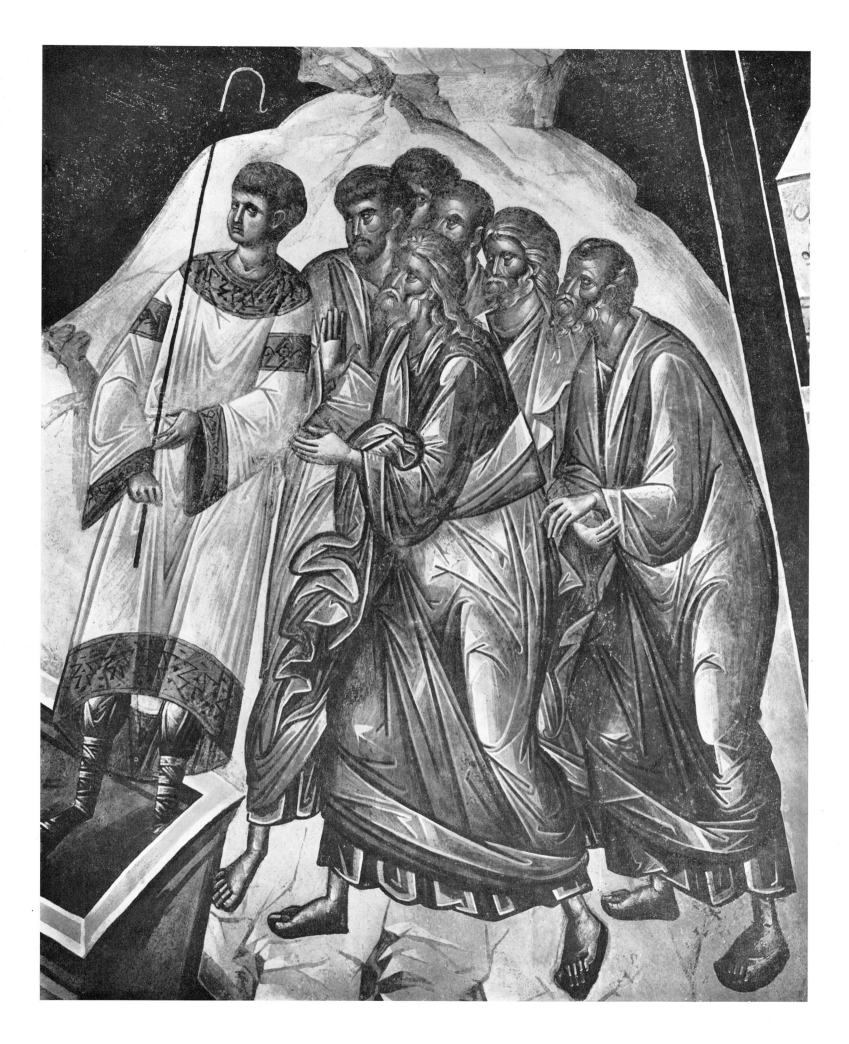

The Anastasis. Detail: the righteous at the right

[201]

The Anastasis. Detail: head of Abel

[201]

The Anastasis. Detail: heads of the righteous at the right

[201]

The Anastasis. Detail: Satan

[201]

The Anastasis. Detail: drapery of Eve's garment

[201]

The Raising of the Widow's Son

[202]

The Raising of the Widow's Son. Detail

[202]

The Raising of the Widow's Son. Detail: head of the widow

[202]

The Raising of the Daughter of Jairus

[203]

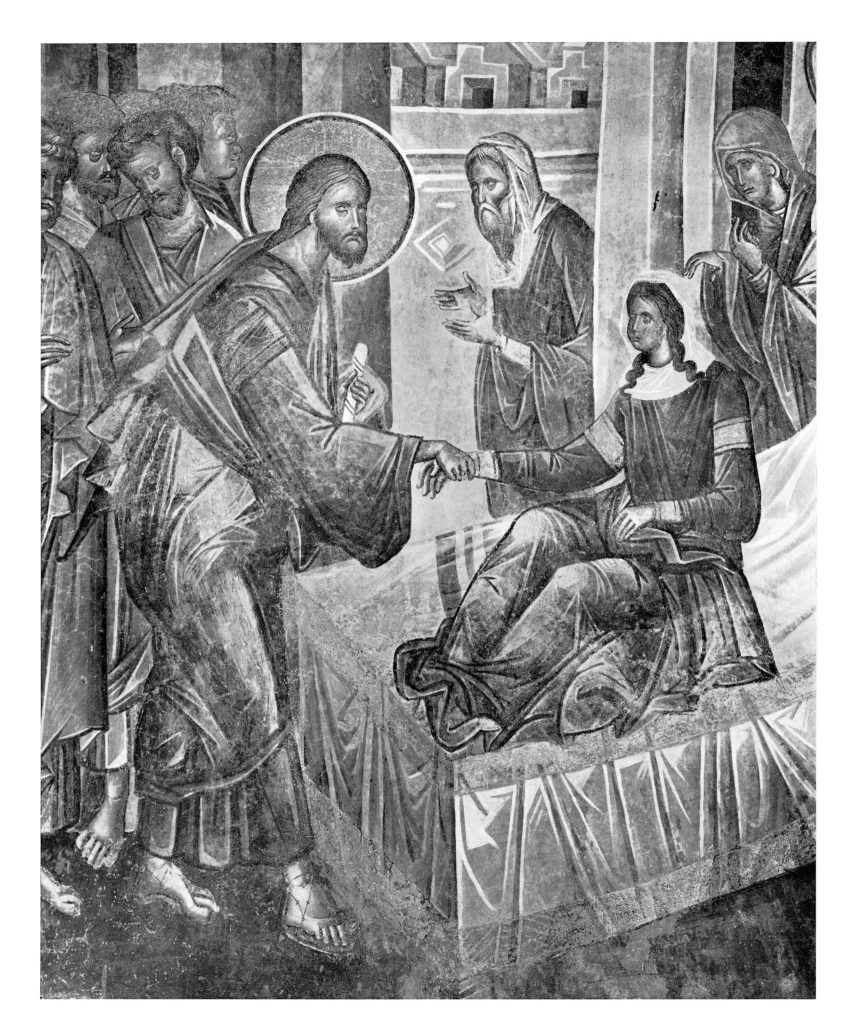

The Raising of the Daughter of Jairus. Detail

[203]

The Raising of the Daughter of Jairus. Detail: Christ, the daughter, and Jairus

[203]

The Raising of the Daughter of Jairus. Detail: heads of disciples

[203]

The Raising of the Daughter of Jairus. Detail: heads of mourning women

[203]

Vaults of the eastern bay

In domical vault: [204]. In pendentives: *upper right*, [205]; *upper left*, [206]; *lower left*,
[207]; *lower right*, [208]. In lunettes: *lower right*, [209]; *left*, [210]; *upper right*, [231]

[204] – [210], [231]

The Last Judgment
Eastern half of the domical vault

[204]

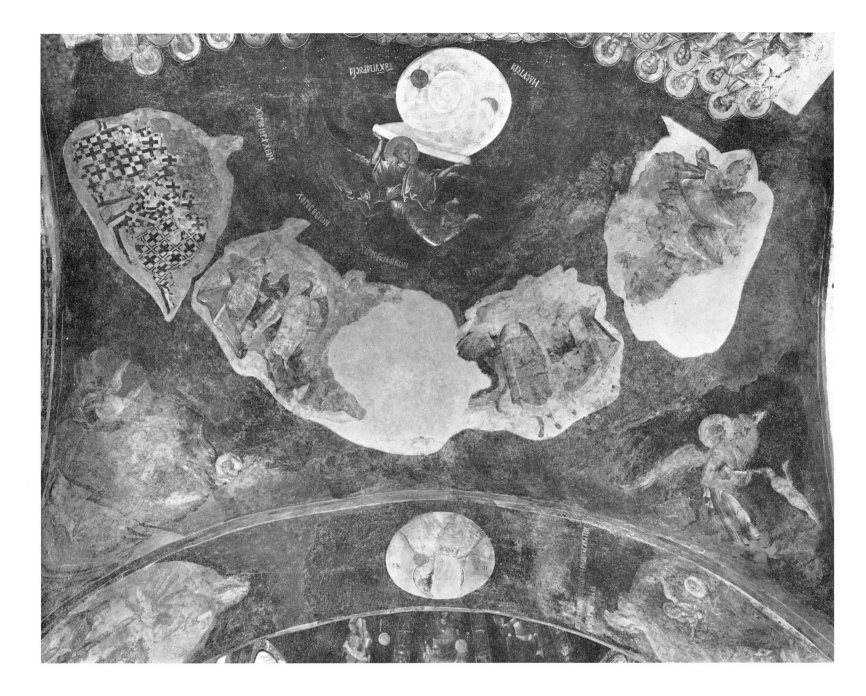

The Last Judgment
Western half of the domical vault

[204]

The Last Judgment
The Scroll of Heaven

[204] - 1

The Last Judgment
The Scroll of Heaven. Detail: the angel

[204] - 1

The Last Judgment
The Deesis and Angels

[204] - 2

The Last Judgment
The Deesis

[204] - 2

The Last Judgment
The Deesis. Detail: bust of Christ

[204] - 2

The Last Judgment
The Apostles, left group

[204] - 2

The Last Judgment
The Apostles, left group. Detail: Apostles 3 and 4

[204] - 2

a

b

c

The Last Judgment
The Apostles, left group. Details: heads
a. Apostle 1   *b*. Apostle 2   *c*. Apostle 5

[204] - 2

a

b

c

The Last Judgment
The Apostles, left group. Details: heads
a. Apostle 3   *b*. Apostle 4   *c*. Apostle 6

[204] - 2

The Last Judgment
Head of an angel

[204] - 2

The Last Judgment
The Apostles, right group

[204] - 2

a

b

c

The Last Judgment
The Apostles, right group. Details: heads
a. Apostle 7   *b.* Apostle 8   *c.* Apostle 11

[204] - 2

a

b

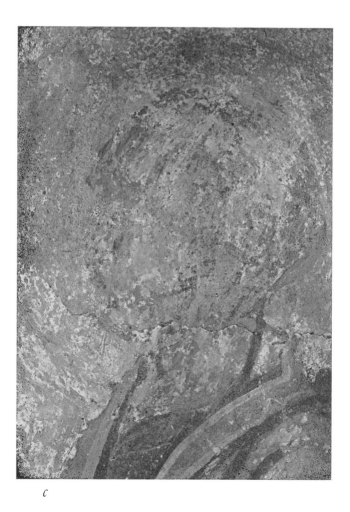

c

The Last Judgment
The Apostles, right group. Details: heads
a. Apostle 9   *b.* Apostle 10   *c.* Apostle 12

[204] - 2

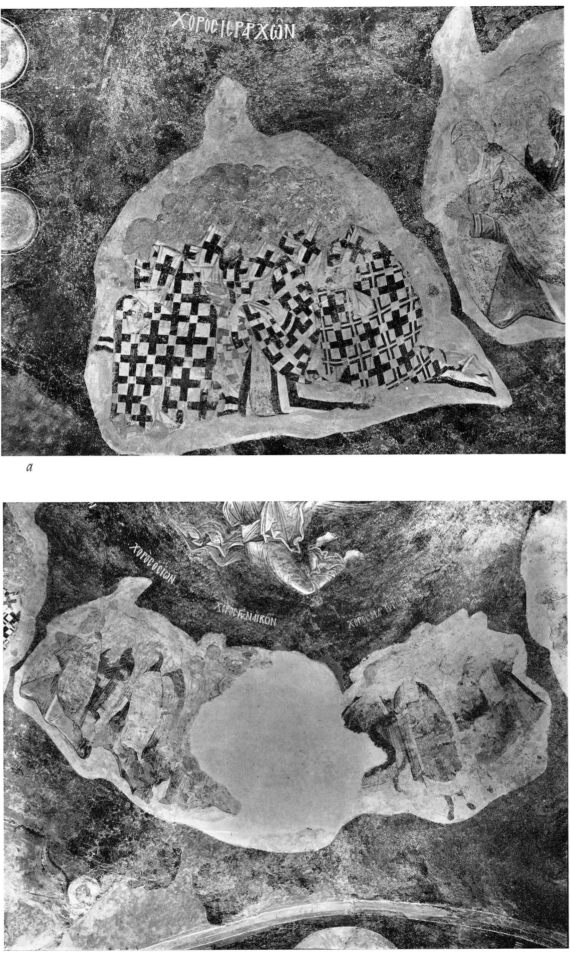

a

b

The Last Judgment
Choirs of the Elect
a. Hierarchs   *b.* Hosioi, Holy Women, Martyrs

[204] - 3

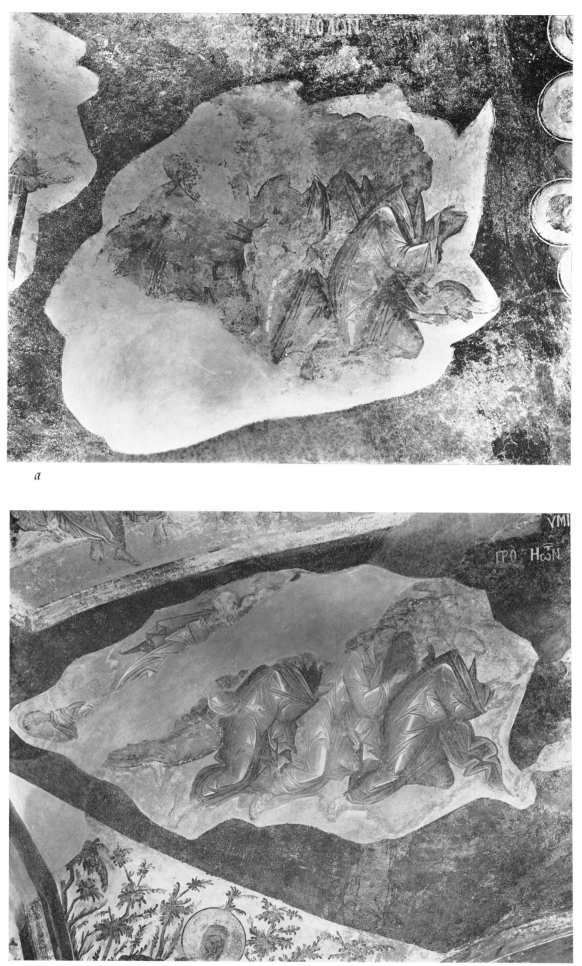

The Last Judgment
Choirs of the Elect
a. Apostles   *b.* Prophets

[204] - 3

The Last Judgment
The Etimasia; The Weighing of Souls
[204] - 4, [204] - 5

The Last Judgment
The Weighing of Souls. Detail: a soul

[204] - 5

The Last Judgment
The Weighing of Souls. Detail: a group of condemned souls

[204] - 5

The Last Judgment
The Weighing of Souls. Detail: souls led into the fire

[204] - 5

The Last Judgment
The Fiery Stream and the Lake of Fire

[204] - 6

The Last Judgment
The Lake of Fire. Detail

[204] - 6

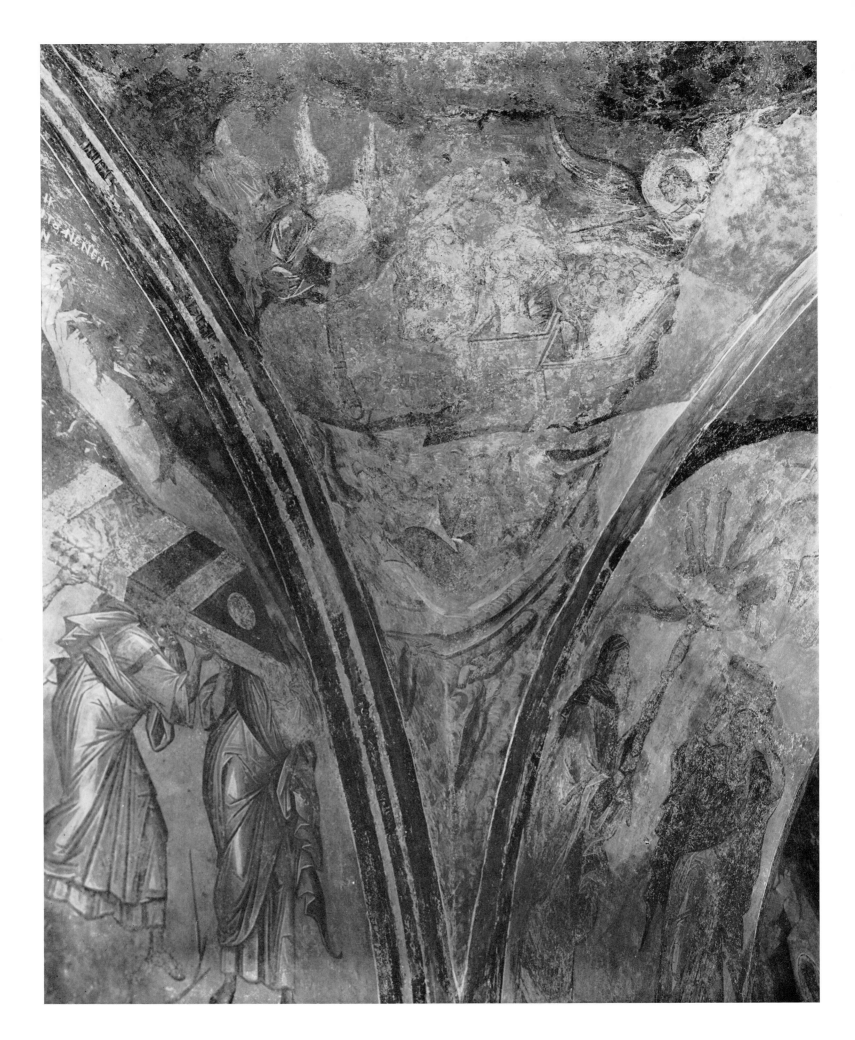

The Last Judgment
The Land and Sea Giving Up Their Dead

[205]

The Last Judgment
An Angel and a Soul

[206]

The Last Judgment
Lazarus the Beggar in Abraham's Bosom

[207]

The Last Judgment
Lazarus the Beggar in Abraham's Bosom. Detail: Lazarus

[207]

The Last Judgment
Lazarus the Beggar in Abraham's Bosom. Detail: souls to the right of Abraham

[207]

The Last Judgment
The Rich Man in Hell

[208]

The Last Judgment
The Torments of the Damned

[209]

The Last Judgment
The Torments of the Damned. Detail: "The Outer Darkness"

[209]

The Last Judgment
The Torments of the Damned. Detail: "The Worm That Sleepeth Not"

[209]

The Last Judgment
The Torments of the Damned. Detail from "The Worm That Sleepeth Not"

[209]

The Last Judgment
The Torments of the Damned. Detail: "The Unquenchable Fire"

[209]

The Last Judgment
The Torments of the Damned. Detail from "The Unquenchable Fire"

[209]

The Last Judgment
The Entry of the Elect into Paradise

[210]

The Last Judgment
The Entry of the Elect into Paradise. Detail: Apostles, the gate of paradise, the Good Thief

[210]

The Last Judgment
The Entry of the Elect into Paradise. Detail: the left half

[210]

The Last Judgment
The Entry of the Elect into Paradise. Detail: the right half

[210]

Vaults of the western bay

In the dome: *center*, [211]; *between the ribs*, [212] – [223]. In the pendentives: *lower left*,
[224]; *lower right*, [225]; *upper right*, [226]; *upper left*, [227]. In the lunette at left:
above, [228]; *below*, [229]. In the lunette at right: *below*, [233]; *above*, [234]

[211] – [229], [233], [234]

Dome of the western bay. The Virgin and attendant angels

[211] – [223]

Dome of the western bay. View from the southwest

The Virgin and Child, medallion of the dome

[211]

First angel

[212]

Second angel

[213]

413

Third angel

[214]

Fourth angel

[215]

Fifth angel

[216]

Sixth angel

[217]

Seventh angel

[218]

Eighth angel

[219]

Ninth angel

[220]

Tenth angel

[221]

Eleventh angel

[222]

Twelfth angel

[223]

Second angel. Detail: head

[213]

Fifth angel. Detail: head

[216]

St. John Damascene, hymnographer

[224]

St. John Damascene, hymnographer. Detail

[224]

St. Cosmas, hymnographer

[225]

St. Cosmas, hymnographer. Detail

[225]

St. Joseph, hymnographer

[226]

St. Joseph, hymnographer. Detail

[226]

St. Theophanes, hymnographer

[227]

Ὁ Ἅ   ΘΕΟΦΆΝΗΣ

St. Theophanes, hymnographer. Detail

[227]

St. Theophanes, hymnographer. Detail: head

[227]

St. Cosmas, hymnographer. Detail: head

[225]

The hymnographers. Details: the inscribed texts

a. The scroll of St. John Damascene [224]   *b.* The codex of St. Cosmas [225]

c. The scroll of St. Joseph [226]   *d.* The codex of St. Theophanes [227]

[224] – [227]

Jacob's Ladder, Jacob Wrestling with the Angel [228]; Moses and the Burning Bush (I) [229]

[228], [229]

Jacob's Ladder; Jacob Wrestling with the Angel

[228]

Jacob's Ladder. Detail: Jacob dreaming

[228]

Jacob's Ladder. Detail: angels ascending and descending

[228]

Jacob's Ladder. Detail: angels descending

[228]

Jacob's Ladder. Detail: Virgin and Child in an arc of heaven

[228]

Jacob Wrestling with the Angel

[228]

Moses and the Burning Bush (I): Moses before the Bush; Moses Removes His Sandals

[229]

Moses and the Burning Bush (I). Detail: Moses before the Bush

[229]

Moses and the Burning Bush (I). Detail: Moses Removes His Sandals

[229]

Moses and the Burning Bush (I). Detail: the flock

[229]

Moses and the Burning Bush (I). Detail: the angel and the Virgin in the burning bush

[229]

a

b

Moses and the Burning Bush (I). Details
a. The angel   *b.* The Virgin

[229]

Moses and the Burning Bush (II): Moses Hides His Face

[230]

Moses and the Burning Bush (II). Detail: Moses

[230]

Moses and the Burning Bush (II). Detail: the angel and the Virgin in the burning bush

[230]

Torments of the Damned [209]; The Bearing of the Ark of the Covenant [231];
below, [250] - [253]

[209], [231], [250] - [253]

ὡς συνετέλεσε Σολομῶ εἰκοδόμησα
τ εκκλησιασεπαντ πρεσβυτω ἰηλεισιωντ ανενεγκ
κιβωτ διαθηκ κυ κπολε δα αυ πε ιων
οἱ ἑρεισ κιβωτ διαθηκη κυ κτοσκη
νωματ μαρτυρι

The Bearing of the Ark of the Covenant

[231]

454

The Bearing of the Ark of the Covenant. Detail

[231]

The Bearing of the Sacred Vessels

[232]

The Bearing of the Sacred Vessels. Detail

[232]

Solomon and All Israel [233]; The Installation of the Ark in the Holy of Holies [234]

[233], [234]

Solomon and All Israel

[233]

The Installation of the Ark in the Holy of Holies

[234]

Isaiah Prophesying; The Angel Smiting the Assyrians before Jerusalem

[235]

Isaiah Prophesying. Detail

[235]

Isaiah Prophesying. Detail: the scroll of Isaiah and the gate of Jerusalem

[235]

The Angel Smiting the Assyrians before Jerusalem. Detail: the angel

[235]

The Angel Smiting the Assyrians before Jerusalem. Detail: the fallen Assyrians

[235]

Aaron and His Sons before the Altar

[236]

Aaron and His Sons before the Altar. Detail: Aaron and his sons

[236]

Aaron and His Sons before the Altar. Detail: the altar

[236]

Western tympanum, showing position of The Souls of the Righteous in the Hand of God.
In crown of arch: the hand and the souls [237]; *lower right:* Unidentified figure [238]

[237], [238]

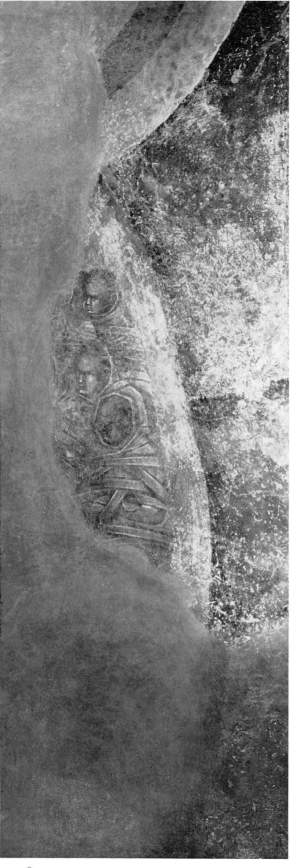

a

b

The Souls of the Righteous in the Hand of God. Details
a. The hand and the souls [237] *b*. Unidentified figure [238]
[237], [238]

a

b

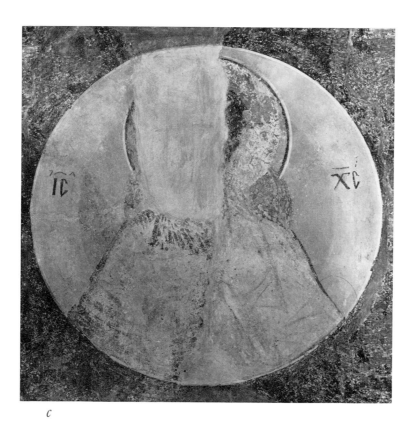

c

Medallion portraits in the arches of the western bay
a. Melchizedek the Righteous [239]   b. Christ [240]   c. Christ [241]
[239] - [241]

Medallion portrait of the Archangel Michael

[242]

Medallion portrait of the Archangel Michael. Detail: head

[242]

Southern wall of the parecclesion. Looking southeast

Southern wall of the parecclesion. Looking southwest

Walls of the apse and bema. Looking southeast

Unidentified church father [243]; St. Athanasius [244]

[243], [244]

St. John Chrysostom

[245]

478

St. Basil

[246]

ΒΑCΙ ΛΟ C Ο 'ΓΓΗ Ο Δ ΓΗΓΟ ΡΟC Ο ΘΕΟΛΟ ΓΟ C Ο 'ΓΗ Ο Δ

St. Gregory the Theologian

[247]

Ο ΘΕΟΛΟΓΟ͂C   Ο ΑΓΙ   ΚΎΡΙΛΟC

St. Cyril of Alexandria

[248]

St. John Chrysostom. Detail: head

[245]

St. Basil. Detail: head

[246]

St. Gregory the Theologian. Detail: head

[247]

St. Cyril of Alexandria. Detail: head

[248]

The Virgin Eleousa

[249]

The Virgin Eleousa. Detail: bust, with Christ Child

[249]

St. George

[250]

Ο Α ΓΕѠΡΓΟϹ

St. George. Detail

[250]

Medallion portrait of St. Florus

[251]

Medallion portrait of St. Laurus

[252]

St. Demetrius

[253]

St. Demetrius. Detail: bust

[253]

St. Theodore Tiro

[254]

St. Theodore Tiro. Detail

[254]

St. Theodore Stratelates

St. Theodore Stratelates. Detail

[255]

St. Mercurius

[256]

St. Mercurius. Detail: head

[256]

St. Procopius [257]; St. Sabas Stratelates [258]

[257], [258]

St. Procopius. Detail: head

[257]

St. Sabas Stratelates. Detail: bust

[258]

St. Sabas Stratelates. Detail: head

[258]

An unidentified saint

[259]

An unidentified saint. Detail: bust

[259]

St. David of Thessalonike

[260]

St. David of Thessalonike. Detail: bust

[260]

St. Eustathius

[261]

St. Eustathius. Detail: bust

[261]

St. Samonas [262]; St. Gurias [263]

[262], [263]

St. Samonas [262]; St. Gurias [263]. Detail

[262], [263]

St. Samonas. Detail: head

[262]

St. Gurias. Detail: head

[263]

St. Artemius or St. Nicetas

[264]

St. Artemius or St. Nicetas. Detail: bust

[264]

Medallion portrait of St. Bacchus

[265]

Medallion portrait of St. Sergius

[266]

St. Sergius [266]; an unidentified military saint [267]; medallion portrait of an unidentified saint [268]

[266] - [268]

An unidentified military saint. Detail

[267]

An unidentified stylite saint

[269]

THE
PASTOPHORIA
AND
PASSAGEWAYS

The prothesis
The dome

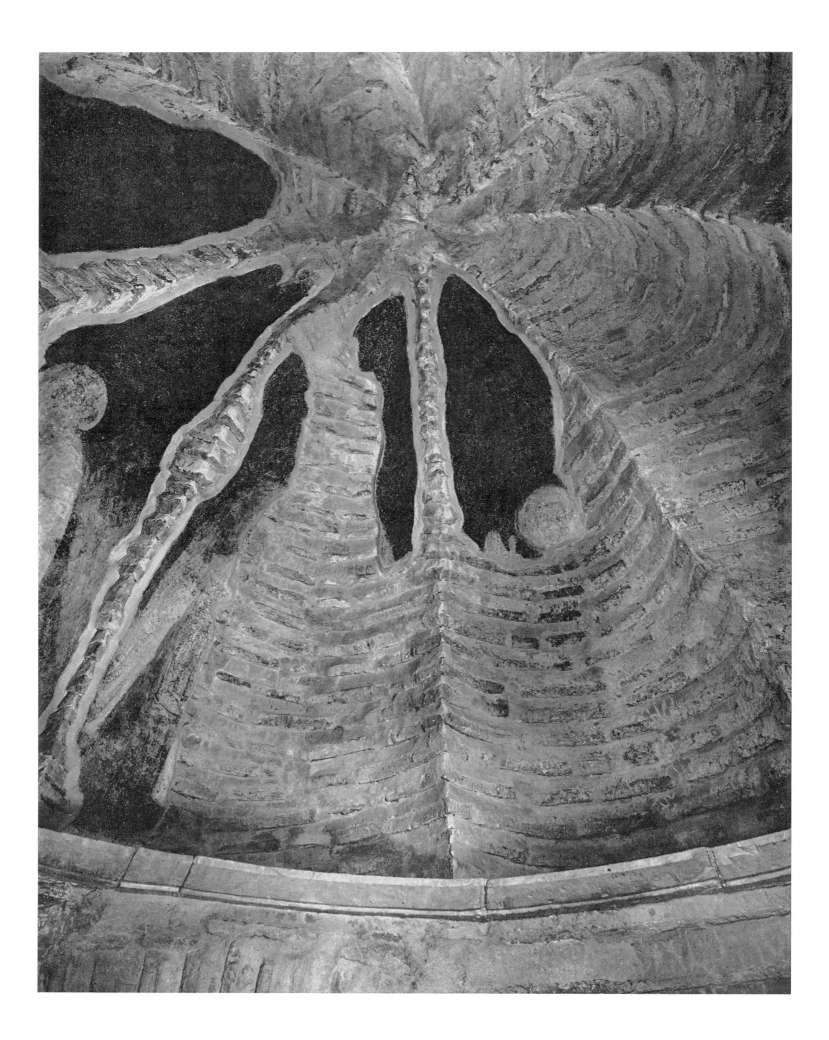

The prothesis
The dome. Angels in flutes 1 and 2

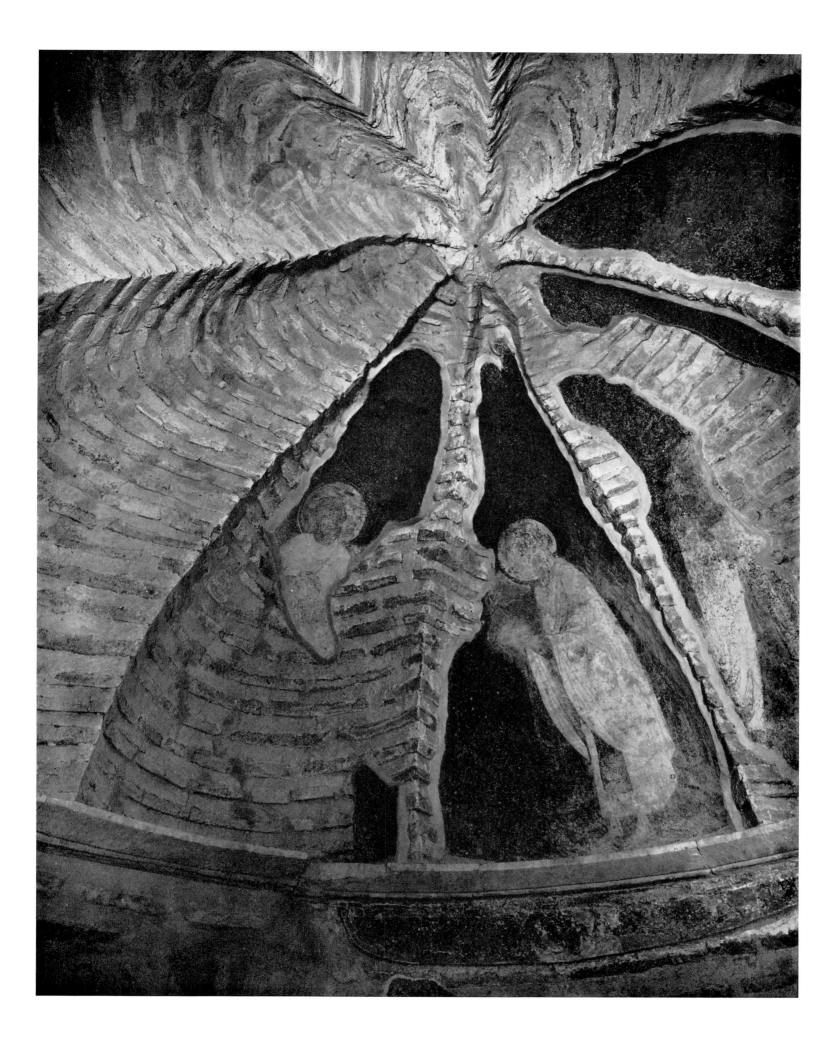

The prothesis
The dome. Angels in flutes 7 and 8

The prothesis
Looking northeast. In conch of apse, the *Amnos*; in pendentive, a seraph;
on north wall, two bishops; in niche, ornaments

The diaconicon
The dome

The diaconicon
The dome. Apostles in segments 7, 8, 1, 2, and 3, from upper left

The diaconicon
The dome. Apostles in segments 8, 1, 2, and 3, from upper left

The diaconicon
The dome. Figures in two zones of segment 6

The diaconicon
Fresco decoration in the soffit of the arch, north wall (twelfth century?)

The northern passageway. Looking east

a

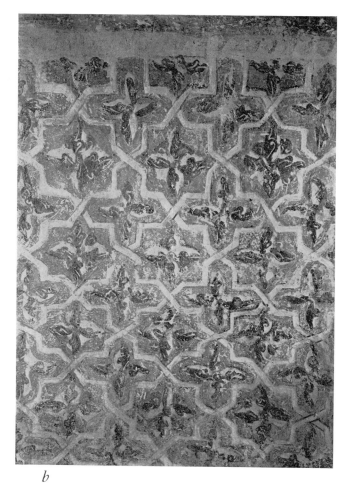

b

c

The northern passageway. Painted ornaments
a. Pattern in the soffit of the barrel vault, east end   *b.* Pattern in the soffit of the barrel vault, west end
c. Ornament on the east wall

a

b

c

Passageway from the parecclesion to the nave
a. The passageway, looking north *b.* Painted ornament in the barrel vault
c. Marbleized panels on the wall

THE
SEPULCHRAL MONUMENTS

a

b

North wall of the parecclesion
a. Tomb A, western bay   *b.* Tomb B, eastern bay

Tomb C (south wall of parecclesion, eastern bay)

Tomb C. Portraits on the back wall

a

b

c

Tomb C. Paintings in the arch soffit
a. Christ, center   *b*. Angel and ornaments, east side   *c*. Angel and ornaments, west side

Tomb D (south wall of parecclesion, western bay), the tomb of Michael Tornikes

Tomb D. Mosaic and fresco portraits on the back wall

Tomb D. Mosaics in the arch soffit
a. Cross in medallion, center   *b.* Tornikes as the monk Makarios, east side
c. The wife of Tornikes as the nun Eugenia, west side

Tomb E (outer narthex, fifth bay), the tomb of Irene Raoulaina Palaeologina

Tomb E. Portraits on the back wall
a. The portraits   *b*. Detail: central figure

a   *b*

Tomb E. Portraits in the jambs
a. A monk, south jamb   *b*. The nun Athanasia, north jamb

Tomb E. Virgin and Child, in the arch soffit, center

Tomb E. Medallion portrait of St. Cosmas, hymnographer, in the arch soffit, south side

Tomb E. Medallion portrait of St. John Damascene, hymnographer, in the
arch soffit, north side

Tomb F (outer narthex, fourth bay)

Tomb F. Portraits on the back wall

Tomb G (outer narthex, second bay)

Tomb G. Painting on the back wall: the deceased standing before the enthroned
Virgin and Child

Tomb H (inner narthex, north wall), the tomb of Demetrius

Tomb H. Mosaics on the back wall: The Virgin of the Source; the crown
of Demetrius (*left*); inscriptions

a

b

Tomb H
a. View of mosaic fragments   *b.* Mosaic in the arch soffit: Christ the Land of the Living

Tomb H. Preliminary sketch of a saint on the first coat of plaster, in the arch soffit, east side

Iconographic Index

Iconographic Index

Bracketed numbers are those assigned to the mosaic and fresco subjects, in an order corresponding with the iconographic sequence of the subjects in the church; the same order is followed in the present volumes. Numbers not in brackets refer to the plates in Vols. 2 and 3. PL. 1–334 (mosaics) are in Vol. 2, PL. 335–553 (frescoes and tombs) in Vol. 3.

Plans and Sections

Fig. 1. General plan of the Kariye Djami

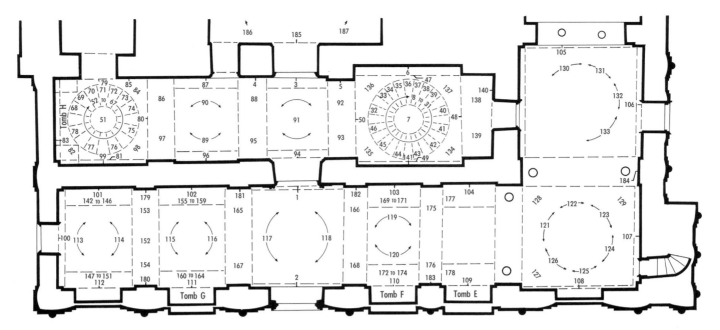

Fig. 2. Plan of the outer and inner narthexes

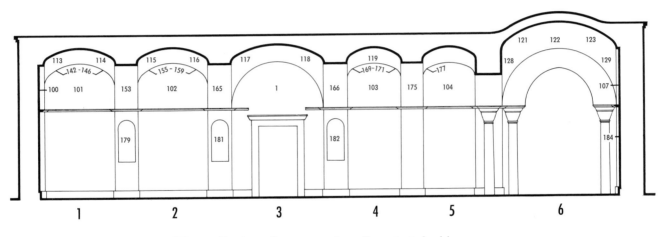

Fig. 3. Section of outer narthex, Bays 1–6, looking east

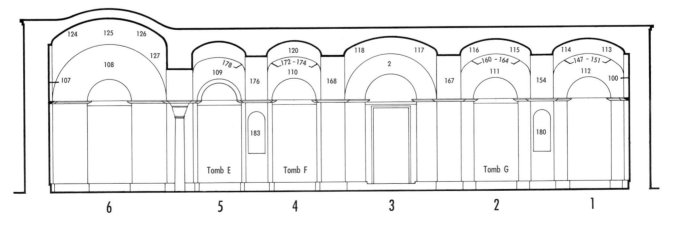

Fig. 4. Section of outer narthex, Bays 1–6, looking west

THE NARTHEXES

Key numbers in red indicate location of mosaics

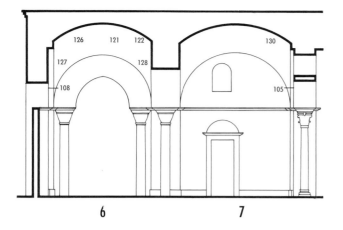

Fig. 5. Section of outer narthex, Bays 6 and 7,
looking north

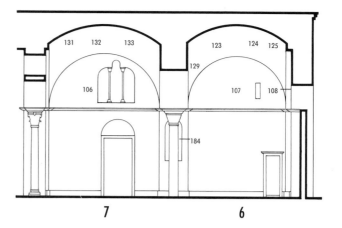

Fig. 6. Section of outer narthex, Bays 6 and 7,
looking south

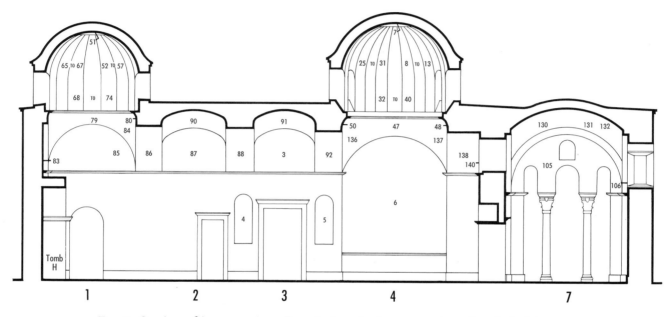

Fig. 7. Section of inner narthex, Bays 1–4, and of outer narthex, Bay 7, looking east

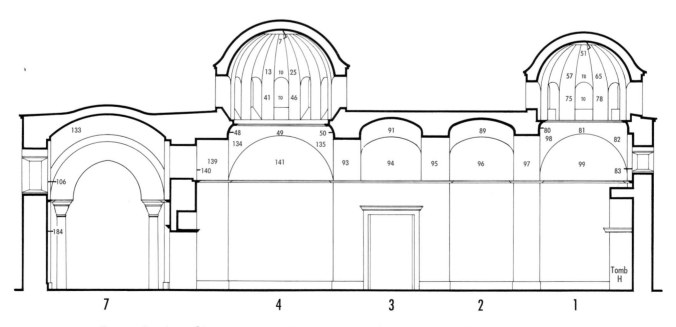

Fig. 8. Section of inner narthex, Bays 1–4, and of outer narthex, Bay 7, looking west

THE NARTHEXES

Key numbers in red indicate location of mosaics

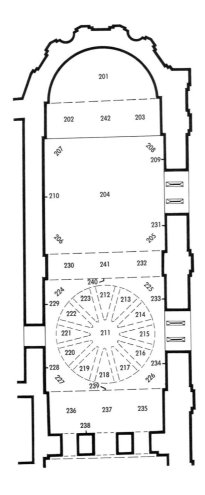

Fig. 9. Plan of the upper zone

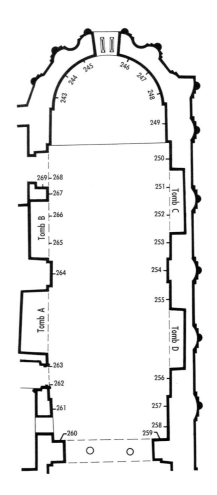

Fig. 10. Plan of the lower zone

THE PARECCLESION

Key numbers in red indicate location of frescoes

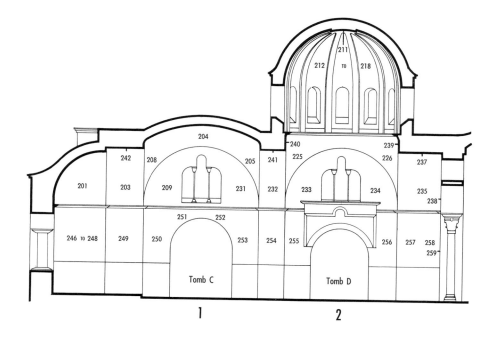

Fig. 11. Section, looking south

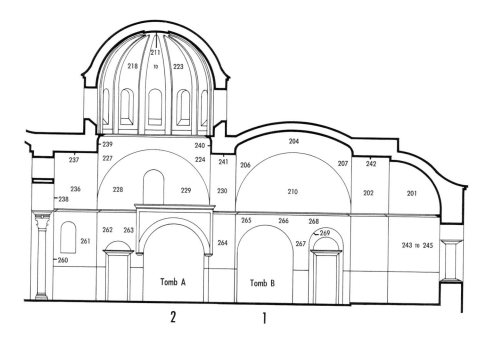

Fig. 12. Section, looking north

THE PARECCLESION

Key numbers in red indicate location of frescoes

THE ENGRAVINGS WERE MADE BY WALKER ENGRAVING CORPORATION, NEW YORK, AND PRINTED BY DAVIS, DELANEY, INC., NEW YORK.

The color plates in these volumes were reproduced from Ektachrome and Kodachrome transparencies taken over many years and under difficult conditions. The publishers wish to express their gratitude to the staff of Walker Engraving Corporation for the exceptional care and attention they devoted to manufacturing the engravings and making many subsequent corrections, and to the staff of Davis, Delaney, Inc. for their painstaking control of the presswork.

THE CAPTIONS WERE COMPOSED BY BAXTER & SPENCER, INC., NEW YORK. KINGSPORT PRESS, INC., KINGSPORT, TENNESSEE, COMPOSED AND PRINTED THE FRONT AND END MATTERS AND BOUND THE VOLUME.